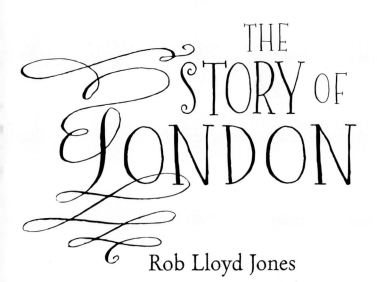

THE STORY OF LONDON

Rob Lloyd Jones

Designed by Karen Tomlins

History consultants: the curatorial
staff of the Museum of London

Reading consultant: Alison Kelly

Edited by Jane Chisholm
Photographic manipulation by Keith Furnival

First published in 2016 by Usborne Publishing Ltd., Usborne House, 83-85 Saffron Hill,
London EC1N 8RT, England. www.usborne.com Copyright © 2016 Usborne Publishing Ltd.

Acknowledgements

© AKG-IMAGES pp8-9, (Bildarchiv Monheim), p12 (North Wind Picture Archives) p31 (Quint
& Lox), p51; © ALAMY p19 (Heritage Image Partnership Ltd), pp20-21 (Mooch Travel), p21 (Liszt
Collection), p25 (Mary Evans Picture Library), p29 (The Art Archive), p30 (Pictorial Press Ltd),
p42 (Mary Evans Picture Library), p43 (Mary Evans Picture Library), p52(b) (Lordprice Collection),
p58 (Kathy deWitt), p59 (Paul Brown); © BRIDGEMAN IMAGES front cover (Lobkowicz Palace,
Prague Castle, Czech Republic), title page (Private Collection/Archives Charmet), p5 (Private
Collection/The Stapleton Collection), p13 (Musee de la Tapisserie, Bayeux, France/With special
authorisation of the city of Bayeux), p17 (British Library, London, UK/© British Library Board. All
Rights Reserved), p18 (Bibliotheque Royale de Belgique, Brussels, Belgium), pp22-23 (© Devonshire
Collection, Chatsworth/Reproduced by permission of Chatsworth Settlement Trustees), p26
(Sunderland Museum & Winter Gardens, Tyne & Wear, UK), p27(t) (Antony House, Cornwall,
UK / National Trust Photographic Library/John Hammond), p27(b) (Musee de Picardie, Amiens,
France), p28 (Private Collection/The Stapleton Collection), p34 (London Metropolitan Archives,
City of London), p35 (Yale Center for British Art, Paul Mellon Collection, USA), pp36-37 (Private
Collection/Photo © Agnew's, London), p37(t) (Universal History Archive/UIG), pp38-39 (Private
Collection), pp44-45 (Private Collection/The Stapleton Collection), pp46-47 (© Leicester Arts &
Museums), p53 (Private Collection/© Look and Learn/Illustrated Papers Collection); © CORBIS
p20(t) (Gustavo Tomsich), p24 (Michael Nicholson), p40 (Burstein Collection), p54, p55, p56, p57
(Bettmann), pp62-63 (Paul Hardy); © FOTOLIBRA p61 (Malcolm Warrington); © GETTY p55 (John
Parrot/Stocktrek Images), p57 (The National Archives/SSPL); © ISTOCK p62 (Alphotographic);
© MARY EVANS PICTURE LIBRARY cover spine, p4 (Iberfoto), p16 (Historic England); p60
(Illustrated London News); © MUSEUM OF LONDON p2-3, p6, p7 (Peter Froste), p9, p10, p11,
pp14-15, p15(t), p22(t), p24(t), pp32-33, p39(t), p41, p48, p49, p50.

The previous page shows the North Bank
of the River Thames, around the year 1920.

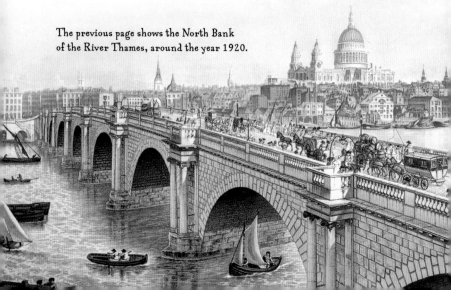

Contents

This view of London, from 1802, shows Blackfriars Bridge crowded with carts and carriages.

Chapter 1

Romans rule

The shrill blast of a trumpet frightened crows from trees and sent a wild boar squealing from a gorse bush. The ground trembled as 40,000 soldiers marched towards the river. It was the year 43AD, and the Roman army was invading Britain.

At the head of the army, a war elephant stomped and snorted through the marshes, its curled tusks slicing the misty air. Behind, a gold eagle – the symbol of Rome – glinted in the sunlight.

The Romans already ruled lands that stretched across what is now Europe. But Emperor Claudius wanted to add *Britannia* (Britain) to his Empire.

Left: A marble sculpture showing Roman soldiers dressed for battle
Above: The head of Emperor Claudius I on a Roman medallion

Marching from the south coast, the Roman army defeated local tribes that tried to defend their land. Only one thing stopped the soldiers' march – a river.

This plaque, from around 300AD, has the first known use of the word *Londiniensi* – Londoners.

The river was wide, with mosquito-infested swamps to the south, and thickly wooded hills rising from the north.

The Romans named it *Tamesa*, the flowing one. They set up camp on the bank, where the river was deep enough for ships to arrive from the sea, bringing supplies from other parts of the Empire.

The river's north bank was a perfect spot for a settlement, with raised, solid ground for building. The Romans built a wooden bridge, timber houses, and shops that opened onto paved streets. They named the town *Londinium*, after an old tribal name for the area.

Londinium grew into a small but prosperous place. Romans mixed with people from local tribes, and traders settled there, excited by new opportunities. Ships brought spices from the Middle East, as well as oil and fish from Italy and Spain.

There was no fort, or wall to defend the town. The people of Londinium thought they were safe in their new home. But they were wrong.

A scene showing how Londinium probably looked around the year 50AD

In the year 60AD, savage battle cries rang around the hills beyond the town. Around 120,000 warriors charged for Londinium.

Leading the attack was Queen Boudicca, flame-haired leader of the Iceni, a tribe from eastern England. Boudicca despised the Romans, who had seized her kingdom and abused her daughters. She was out for revenge.

"Let's show the Romans they are hares trying to rule over wolves!" she screamed.

Boudicca rides her chariot in this statue that overlooks the River Thames in Central London.

A lot of the town's population had fled. Those that remained were shown no mercy. Some were dragged from their homes and slaughtered in the street. Others were hanged or crucified. Boudicca's warriors pushed burning hay wagons down the streets, setting fire to buildings.

Boudicca was finally defeated by the Roman army, but Londinium was in ruins.

Londinium had never been a big town. It was just a speck in the vast Roman Empire. Fifty years later, all that had changed.

By then, the town had been rebuilt in a much grander style, with a bustling forum (market place) and an oval amphitheatre, where crowds watched wild beast hunts or – on special occasions – gladiators fight to the death.

Lavish mosaics like this decorated the homes of wealthy Romans in Londinium.

From around the year 200, Londinium was protected by an imposing stone wall, with six guarded gateways.

The town's population grew to around 45,000, a mix of traders and their families, soldiers, craftsmen and shop workers. A small settlement grew on the south bank of the river too, an area known as Southwark.

It was a bright time for the bustling Roman town. But things would soon turn dark again.

A model of Londinium's bustling riverbank around the year 100

This ornate brooch, found in a grave in London, was probably worn by a wealthy Saxon noble.

Chapter 2

Saxons and Vikings

"Prepare to march!" barked the Roman governor, stomping through Londinium to gather his soldiers.

It was the year 410, and the Roman Empire was crumbling. Soldiers were needed to defend Roman lands in Europe from barbarian tribes.

It was grim news for Londinium. With the Empire in trouble, traders had left to seek opportunities elsewhere. Houses were abandoned. Mosaics overgrew with weeds. By 450, Londinium was a ghost town.

But the town's position on the river was simply too good for it to stay empty. Around the year 600, tribes from Germany, the Saxons, settled in an area west of the Roman walls. They called their settlement *Lundenwic* (*wic* meant 'market place').

As Saxon Lundenwic grew wealthy, it became a target...

In 851, a fleet of Viking battle ships sailed up the Thames. The Danish warriors charged into Lundenwic like animals. They set fire to the houses and slaughtered anyone they saw.

For over 150 years, London was a battleground for fights between Saxons and Vikings, until the town returned to Saxon control.

A fleet of Viking ships in attack mode

In 1042, the Saxon King Edward the
Confessor ordered a palace to be built
up-river from London, in a swampy area called
Westminster. A monastery was established there
too, and its church – Westminster Abbey – was
completed in 1065. From then on, Westminster
became the home of English kings and queens.

A tapestry scene showing Westminster Abbey soon after it was built

On Christmas Day, 1066, Duke William of
Normandy was crowned king in Wesminster
Abbey. To strengthen his control, William 'the
Conquerer' built three castles in London.

The largest, on the town's eastern edge, had
a stone keep (tower) washed with white lime,
called the White Tower. It was the first part of
a much larger fortification that would become
known as the Tower of London.

Chapter 3

The Middle Ages

In 1209, the last stone was laid on a new bridge across the River Thames. London Bridge was an spectacular sight, with nineteen stone arches, a drawbridge, and houses and shops lining the route from the north bank to Southwark in the south. The bridge even had a stone chapel halfway across, where people could stop and pray as they crossed the river.

The chapel was one of over a hundred churches in London. During the Middle Ages (from around 1200 to 1500), the church owned the most land in the city, including a dozen monasteries, where monks lived and prayed.

A wax seal from around 1250, showing St. Paul and the City of London

The grandest church by far was St. Paul's Cathedral. The cathedral's 120m (400ft) spire could be seen from all over the city.

This view of London around the year 1400 shows the Tower of London on the right, St. Paul's Cathedral on the left, and London Bridge crossing the Thames.

The city's narrow, twisting streets buzzed with activity. Tailors worked on Threadneedle Street, bakeries lined Bread Street, and cows were kept in pens on Milk Street.

Each industry had its own Guild, a group that set prices for buying and selling. Some, such as the Merchant Tailors and the Goldsmiths, became very powerful. Their leaders met at the city's imposing Guildhall, where every year they elected London's new Mayor.

London's Guildhall as it looked around the year 1450

London got bigger and richer, but dirtier too. The crowded streets were awash with animal dung, waste from chamber pots, and vegetable peel thrown from market stalls.

Diseases spread quickly among the filth. In November 1348, a devastating plague reached London from Europe. Dark pustules grew on victims' bodies, which later gave the disease its name – the Black Death.

A priest blesses boil-covered victims of the Black Death, in this scene from a medieval manuscript.

The Black Death ravaged London for seven months, killing half its population – around 40,000 people. Pale, twisted corpses were heaped into carts and buried in 'plague pits' on the edges of the city.

It would take over 150 years for London's population to reach the size it had been before the Black Death. And the disease wasn't really gone. Plague would return to London, only next time would be even worse...

The scene below shows victims of the Black Death being laid in 'plague pits'. The corpses are in coffins, although most were simply wrapped in cloth.

Chapter 4
Tudor Times

cross London, soldiers thumped on monastery doors. "Open up!" they roared. "By order of King Henry!"

It was 1540. King Henry VIII, the second of the Tudor family of rulers, had declared himself Supreme Head of the Church in England. Everything the church owned was now his, and he wanted it *all*.

London's monasteries were torn down, and new buildings rose in their place. Bishops' palaces were given to nobles, in exchange for loyalty to the King.

Above: The earliest map to show all of London, printed in Germany in 1574

19

For Henry, London was a place to show off his wealth and power. In Westminster, an old royal residence was turned into a huge new palace called Whitehall, where Henry hosted sumptuous feasts and jousting contests.

Henry VIII

The King built another lavish palace in Greenwich, called *Placentia*, and gained an even grander home in the countryside west of London when he siezed Hampton Court from his advisor Cardinal Wolsey.

The imposing entrance to Hampton Court Palace, lined with statues of animals called 'the Kings's Beasts'

New buildings were added to the Tower of London, too. The castle became feared as a prison, where enemies of the King were locked up.

Prisoners who arrived at the Tower by boat through 'Traitors' Gate' knew they might never leave. On 17 May, 1536, Henry's second wife, Anne Boleyn, had her head chopped off in the Tower courtyard, by order of the King.

A boat approaches Traitors' Gate, carrying a prisoner into the Tower of London.

From 1500 to 1600, London's population grew four times larger, to around 200,000. Crammed among the winding streets were button makers and book binders, saddle makers and goldsmiths – dozens of trades and crafts.

London Bridge was more spectacular than ever, lined with the tall, elegant homes of rich merchants. Below, hundreds of ferries carried passengers back and forth across the river.

London Bridge as it looked around 1640

On the south bank of the Thames, Southwark flourished too. During the reign of Henry VIII's daughter, Elizabeth I (1558-1603), the area turned into London's playground.

People flocked there to gamble on cock fights and bear baiting (watching bears fight dogs), which were both banned within the City of London's walls.

But Southwark was best-known for its playhouses. Rich and poor came across the river to watch acting companies perform in three large playhouses: the Rose, the Swan and the Globe.

Up to 3,000 people squeezed into each, sitting in circular galleries or standing in an open air 'yard' in front of the stage. They jeered and cheered, and sometimes hurled rotten fruit at the actors on stage.

Church towers and spires rise all over London, in this view from around 1650.

Today, by far the best known Elizabethan playwright is William Shakespeare. Shakespeare moved to London from Stratford-upon-Avon around 1590, and became a part-owner of the Globe. He

William Shakespeare

wrote at least 36 plays, most of which were performed there for the first time. They included the tale of doomed lovers Romeo and Juliet, and the tragedy of a Danish Prince, called Hamlet.

None of Shakespeare's plays are set entirely in London. But the city influenced them all, with its hustle and bustle, rowdy events, and dazzling displays of royal power.

This drawing, from 1647, shows the Globe Theatre tucked among the houses and inns of Southwark.

Here are the eight 'Gunpowder plotters' that tried
to kill the King. Guy Fawkes is shown in the middle.

Chapter 5

Plots, wars and plague

*I*n the middle of the night on November 5,
1605, a man hid in a London cellar with
thirty-six barrels of gunpowder.

His name was Guy Fawkes, and the cellar was
beneath the Houses of Parliament. Fawkes and
a gang of Catholic plotters planned to blow up
Parliament when England's new Protestant king,
James I, appeared there the next day.

But the Gunpowder Plot had been discovered.

Soldiers stormed into the cellar and dragged Fawkes from hiding. He was taken to the Tower of London and tortured for three days.

On January 31, 1606, Fawkes and seven of his gang were dragged behind a horse to Westminster. They were hanged and their bodies were cut into quarters. Their heads were stuck on spikes over London Bridge, as grisly warnings to any other traitors lurking in the city.

The moment that royal guards captured Guy Fawkes in a cellar beneath the Houses of Parliament

Forty-three years later, in 1649, another famous execution took place in Westminster. It was the final scene of a fierce Civil War that had divided the country, as supporters of King Charles I fought the army of Parliament.

King Charles I

The King lost. On January 30, he climbed onto a scaffold and sank to his knees. A deep groan rushed through the crowd as the executioner swung his axe, slicing off the King's head.

King Charles I kneels on a scaffold, as a crowd watches his execution in Westminster.

Only 11 years later, cannons fired in celebration at the Tower of London as England's new king, Charles II, rode in ceremony to the Palace of Whitehall.

London was an even grander city than it had been under the Tudors. In 1630, architect Inigo Jones had designed its first large public square, Covent Garden.

New streets were built over meadows, and lined with fashionable shops. Parks once used by kings and queens for hunting were opened to the public. Hyde Park and St. James's Park became fashionable places to be seen.

A view of Inigo Jones's elegent new piazza (square) in Covent Garden, in 1647

But the larger London grew, the dirtier it became. Rats thrived among the waste. And where there were rats there was disease...

In the summer of 1665, plague returned to London. The 'Great Plague' of 1665 was the last major outbreak of the disease in the city, and one of the worst. Men pushed carts along the streets, calling, "Bring out your dead!"

Londoners carry plague corpses from their city, as the skeleton figure of Death watches, in this scene from a 1666 broadsheet (an early version of a newspaper).

Victims were locked in their houses to die. Red crosses were painted on their doors as warnings, with the words, 'Lord have mercy upon us.'

Thousands of Londoners, including King Charles and his court, fled the city. Among those who stayed was Samuel Pepys, who worked for the Navy. Pepys watched in horror, and recorded what he saw in his diary.

'Lord, how empty the streets are, and melancholy, so many poor sick people in the streets, full of sores...'

By the time the Great Plague ended, in the winter of 1665, the disease had killed between 60,000 and 100,000 Londoners. The city barely had time to recover before another disaster struck...

An illustration, from around the time of the Great Plague, showing bodies being laid in graves outside London

Chapter 6
The Great Fire

Early in the morning on 2 September, 1666, a servant woke the Mayor of London, Thomas Bludworth.

"Sir," he gasped. "There's a fire, in the middle of the city."

Bleary eyed and tired, the Mayor glanced out the window. Smoke rose somewhere in the heart of the city. "Pish!" he scoffed, as he crawled back into bed. He thought the fire would be easily put out.

The Mayor was wrong.

The Great Fire of London began at a baker's shop on Pudding Lane, near London Bridge. It had been a dry summer, so flames spread fast among the tightly-packed timber buildings. Fanned by strong easterly winds, they were soon beyond control.

People scramble into boats to escape the Great Fire, as flames approach St. Paul's Cathedral.

Fearing the fire might reach the Tower of London, where gunpowder was stored, King Charles rode through the smoke-drenched streets, urging everyone to fight the flames.

Chains of people passed buckets of water from the river, while others battled the flames with water squirts. Teams of men pulled down buildings with hooks and ropes, hoping to stop the fire from spreading.

Londoners gather with their belongings outside the Tower of London, as their city burns.

On the third day of the fire, St. Paul's Cathedral was swallowed by flames. The lead on the Cathedral's roof melted. Glowing red, it trickled like lava along the streets.

The Great Fire of London raged for four days, until the wind died down and the flames stopped spreading. As the smoke cleared, Samuel Pepys described the scene as, "the saddest sight of desolation that I ever saw."

Only eight people died in the fire, but over 13,000 houses were destroyed. Around 100,000 people were left homeless, camping in fields around the city.

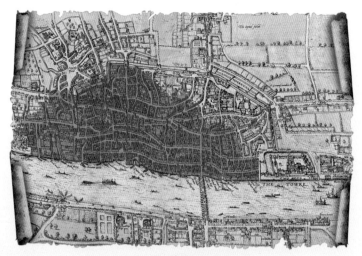

The red area on this map of London shows how far the fire spread in four days.

For some, the charred remains of London presented an exciting opportunity. Eager architects drew up plans to rebuild the city, after the King announced he wanted to see, 'a much more beautiful city rise from the ashes.'

But Londoners needed new homes, and fast. So, in the end, most houses were simply rebuilt in the same places. To make the city more fireproof, everything had to be built of brick or stone.

Gifted young architect Christopher Wren was appointed Surveyor of the King's Works. From 1670 to 1686, Wren rebuilt fifty-one churches, as well as large public buildings such as a new Guildhall.

In 1675 Wren began work on a new cathedral for the city. Huge blocks of stone were brought up the Thames by barge. Around 400 masons and craftsmen clambered around scaffolds, hammering and chiselling.

The new St. Paul's Cathedral had an immense stone dome inspired by architecture from Rome. A golden cross rose from its peak.

Nearby, Wren built a stone column topped with a gleaming golden urn. The Monument remembered the Great Fire, but also celebrated the new city that was rising from the ashes.

Christopher Wren's new
St. Paul's Cathedral, in 1754

Chapter 7
Elegance and despair

*L*ondon's population kept growing. By the
end of the the 1700s, it was the first city
in Europe since Ancient Rome to have over a
million people.

Elegant squares were built, framed by tall
townhouses for the rich. New bridges crossed
the Thames, and streets were laid out in
London's fashionable 'West End'. Their shops
sold delicate porcelain, exquisite silks, and
clocks in decorated golden cases. The city's
craftsmen became famous around the world for
the quality of their work.

Several institutions were established in
London that encouraged new ideas in science
and art. Scientists conducted experiments at the

A view along the Thames showing the first stone
bridge at Westminster, which was completed in 1750

The Royal Observatory, in Greenwich Park

Royal Society, astronomers studied the stars from the Royal Observatory in Greenwich, and surgeons cut open corpses in London's anatomy colleges, to learn more about how the body works.

The British Museum opened in 1759, showing off over 50,000 'curiosities' – art and historical artefacts – gathered by the physician Sir Hans Sloane.

On summer evenings, rich Londoners flocked to pleasure gardens: private parks where those able to afford the entrance fee could dance, drink and gossip. At Vauxhall Gardens on the south bank of the Thames, visitors dined in alcoves, or strolled

At the heart of Vauxhall Gardens was the pavillion, were an orchestra played and people gossiped and danced.

among avenues of trees hung with lanterns.

At the annual Bartholomew Fair, near St. Paul's, crowds jostled to see fire eaters and freak shows, jugglers and wild beasts.

Crowds jostle and dance at Bartholomew Fair in Smithfield.

Other fairs were held in Southwark and Greenwich, and a popular fair in May gave its name to the area where it was held – Mayfair. When the Thames froze over in 1740, a 'Frost Fair' was even held on the ice.

This frost fair on the frozen River Thames has food stalls and skating. The artist even shows people driving carriages across the thick ice.

Each year more and more people moved to London from the countryside, to seek work in shops or as servants. As the city's population grew, living conditions got even worse for the poor.

To escape their hard lives, people drank gin – a cheap, addictive

GIN LANE.

Artist William Hogarth created this scene of 'Gin Lane' to warn against the dangers of gin. Addicts lie about the street, or sell their belongings to buy more gin.

drink made from grain. There were around 17,000 'gin houses' in the city – squalid shops or dank basements where people could buy and drink gin.

One politician claimed that, "the whole town of London swarmed with drunken people from morning till night."

In 1751, the government passed an act to control the gin trade. But things for London's poor continued to get worse, as the city kept growing...

Chapter 8
Victorian giant

The river was dark and full of foul slime. Steam barges set off from rickety jetties, their huge wooden paddles churning through raw sewage. Pipes jutted from the river banks, pumping toxic gunk from dozens of factories that lined the banks.

It was the hot summer of 1858, and the River Thames reeked. In the Houses of Parliament, politicians soaked the curtains with chemicals to mask the stench. They called it 'the Great Stink'.

Rickety wharves and warehouses line the banks of the Thames, as steam boats and barges crowd the river.

London was growing too fast and getting too filthy. Ships arrived at new docks along the river, bringing people as well as goods to the city.

People came from Ireland to escape famine, and from all over Europe. Around 100,000 Jews moved to London during the 1800s, from Russia, Poland, Holland and Germany.

London's population doubled between 1800 and 1850, and then doubled again – to around six million – by the end of the century. It was by far the biggest city the world had ever known.

No one knew how to cope with so many people in one place. Waste spilled into the Thames, or bubbled up from cesspits beneath houses, and sloshed around water pumps. Diseases from contaminated water, such as cholera and typhoid, killed thousands. Something had to be done.

THE "SILENT HIGHWAY" - MAN.
"Your MONEY or your LIFE!"

An image from a magazine showing Death rowing along the polluted River Thames

FLEET-STREET.—DEEPENING THE SEWER.

Workers lay new sewers beneath a London street.

The answer came from an engineer named Joseph Bazalgette. From 1859, Bazalgette built a new system of sewers beneath London, a vast network of tunnels and pipes that carried waste from the city and out to sea.

It was one of the most ambitious engineering projects ever, and showed off London as the world's leading city for industry and new ideas.

In 1851, a huge show was held in Hyde Park, to celebrate inventions and industries. Opened by Queen Victoria, *The Great Exhibition of the Works and Industry of All Nations* was staged in the Crystal Palace, a glass structure three times the length of St. Paul's Cathedral.

Around 6 million people visited the Great Exhibition. They marvelled at everything from printing presses to steam engines, ivory thrones from India, and an entire Turkish bazaar. Profits from tickets funded new museums and colleges in London.

In 1840, work began on a new Houses of Parliament, after the old one burned down in a fire. Five years later, the last stones were laid on a new public square built to celebrate a British naval victory against the French, at the Battle of Trafalgar in 1805.

A stone column was erected in the middle of Trafalgar Square, topped with a statue of Admiral Lord Nelson, who had commanded the British fleet.

The Crystal Palace, as it looked after the Great Exhibition, when it was moved from Hyde Park to South London

At the same time, London was being carved up to lay new railway lines, and build train stations. In 1863, the world's first underground trains rattled beneath the city. Passengers in open wagons coughed on the soot from the steam engines.

Now that Londoners could travel further to and from work, the city got even bigger. The wealthy moved to village suburbs such as Clapham in the South, or Primrose Hill in the North.

The wealthiest Londoners kept townhouses in expensive areas of Central London, such as Mayfair or Belgravia. During the 'London season', from May to July, they dressed in their finest silks and satins, and mingled at balls, operas, and parties at the homes of the rich.

Passengers at London's Paddington Station prepare to board a steam train to leave the city.

But as London's rich partied, life for the city's poor grew almost unbearable.

Many of the new railway lines were built through areas of old housing where London's poor had lived in cramped, squalid conditions. Thrown from their homes, those people moved to even more crowded slums in the East End or the middle of the city.

Whole families lived in single rooms, sharing what little food they could afford. Their homes had few windows and very little fresh air.

This scene was drawn to bring attention to the awful conditions in which many Londoners lived, crammed together in small rooms.

People living in slums had no running water, so often took their drinking water from open drains or sewers. Hundreds of people shared a single outdoor toilet. Barefoot children roamed the slums hunting for food.

In 1852, journalist Henry Mayhew visited one of London's slums, and described the appalling conditions he saw.

'The water of the huge ditch in front of the houses is covered with a scum... Along the banks are heaps of indescribable filth... the air has literally the smell of a graveyard.'

Dilapidated wooden houses lean over a polluted canal, in a typical South London slum.

Homeless Londoners huddle together for warmth as they sleep on a pavement.

London's population had grown so large there weren't enough jobs for everyone. In Whitechapel, in the East, 8,000 homeless people shivered in doorways every night.

From the middle of the 1800s, some Londoners campaigned for better living conditions for the poor. Author Charles Dickens was one of the biggest celebrities in the city. He wrote about the hard lives of the poor in novels such as *David Copperfield* and *Oliver Twist*.

By 1870, around half of London's children had no education. Instead they worked, and they worked *hard*. Young chimney sweeps climbed and scrubbed sooty chutes, and mudlarks waded through filth on the Thames riverbanks, digging for anything worth selling.

Thousands of London children toiled as servants or maids, working exhausting days in the homes of the rich.

A young girl sells flowers from a basket in Trafalgar Square.

With few prospects, many of London's poor turned to crime. Gangs of pickpockets swiped purses or silk handkerchiefs. Garrotters strangled victims and stole from their pockets.

In the Autumn of 1888, at least five women were murdered in Whitechapel, in the East End. The killer, nicknamed Jack the Ripper, was never caught.

Any criminal who *was* caught might be sent to notorious Newgate Gaol, or to dreaded 'prison hulks', dank old warships that were anchored off the Thames and turned into floating prisons.

A prison hulk (on the left) moored beside a ship on the River Thames

Executions of murderers were popular events. Crowds of up to 30,000 people cheered and jeered as convicted criminals dangled from a hangman's rope.

PREPARING FOR AN EXECUTION.

An excited crowd gathers outside Newgate Gaol, near
St. Paul's Cathedral, to watch a prisoner being executed.

As London kept growing, its poor kept suffering. Approaching the 20th century, it was still the biggest city in the world. But other countries, especially U.S.A. and Germany, had risen in power, and Britain's supremacy began to decline. That meant London's did too…

Chapter 9

The 20th century...and on

Sirens wailed, and searchlights swept back and forth across the night sky. It was September 7, 1940. Britain was at war with Germany, and London was under attack.

Almost 1,000 German warplanes swarmed over the city, unleashing bombs. Below, buildings collapsed, and fires raged.

The German *Luftwaffe* (air force) bombed London every night for the next 57 days, in a series of raids known as 'the Blitz' (from the German word *Blitzkrieg* – lightning war).

Each night London was engulfed in dark smoke and dust. As bombs exploded, some Londoners scrambled to the safety of small air raid shelters in their gardens.

Others, around 150,000 people, sheltered in the city's underground stations. They huddled together, as the walls shook from the impact of falling bombs.

AIR RAID PRECAUTIONS

KEEP COOL

DON'T RUN

DON'T SCREAM

PREVENT DISORDER

OBEY ALL INSTRUCTIONS

Posters like this encouraged Londoners to stay calm during air raids.

St. Paul's Cathedral engulfed in smoke during a night of the Blitz

The Germans hoped the attacks would force Britain to surrender. In fact, the opposite happened. Londoners refused to give in. Most people tried to get on with their daily lives, picking their way through rubble on their way to work.

But the bombs took their toll. Around 20,000 people were killed, and far more were injured. A million London homes were destroyed or damaged. Huge areas of the city were left as smoking ruins.

Smoke rises from blown-up buildings, in this photograph of the aftermath of air raids near St. Paul's Cathedral.

After the war ended, in 1945, Londoners needed something to celebrate.

In 1948, the city hosted the Olympic Games. A few years later, in 1951, around 8.5 million people visited the Festival of Britain, an exhibition to show off new ideas in science, art and architecture. Two years after that, cheering Londoners lined the streets of Westminster, as a golden carriage carried Queen Elizabeth II to her coronation at Westminster Abbey.

A poster advertising the 1951 Festival of Britain

The Queen's carriage on its way to Westminster Abbey on June 2, 1953

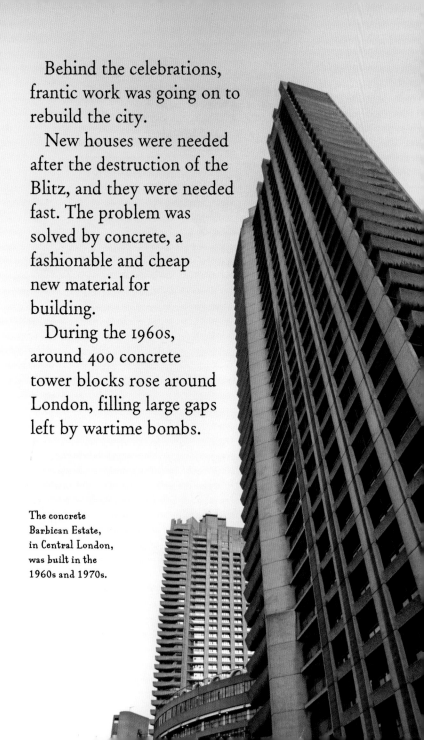

Behind the celebrations, frantic work was going on to rebuild the city.

New houses were needed after the destruction of the Blitz, and they were needed fast. The problem was solved by concrete, a fashionable and cheap new material for building.

During the 1960s, around 400 concrete tower blocks rose around London, filling large gaps left by wartime bombs.

The concrete Barbican Estate, in Central London, was built in the 1960s and 1970s.

Homes were needed too for thousands of people moving to London in search of jobs. People came from all over the world. They came from India, Pakistan and the West Indies. People from Jamaica settled in Notting Hill, in West London. People from Hong Kong created a vibrant new 'Chinatown' in Soho.

Red lanterns decorate the streets of Chinatown during Chinese New Year.

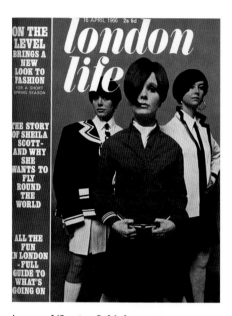

A cover of 'London Life', from 1966, a magazine
that celebrated art, fashion and culture in London.

London's exciting multicultural atmosphere
attracted famous designers and artists to the city.
Fashion designers set up shops in Chelsea, or
Carnaby Street in Soho. London rock bands,
such as The Who and the Rolling Stones had
hits around the globe, and The Beatles - the
best-selling band in history - recorded several
albums in the city. London became a leading
city for music and fashion, the 'style capital'
of the world.

Carnaby Street, in Central London, was one of the city's most fashionable shopping streets during the 1960s.

During the 1980s, East London's old docks were redeveloped into a 'mini city' of glass office towers. The area, known as Docklands, attracted banks and businesses, and grew into one of the world's leading financial districts.

The Olympic Stadium is at the heart of London's
Olympic Park for the 2012 Games.

In 2012, London became the first city to host
the modern Olympic Games for a third time.
A rundown industrial area in Stratford, East
London, was converted into an Olympic Park,
with a stadium that seated 80,000 fans.

Today, London still has lots of problems, but it's one of the world's most exciting places. It now has around 8 million people. Together they speak over 300 languages.

Around 18 million people visit London every year, making it the most popular destination in the world. Tourists gaze at Roman walls, medieval castles, and palaces of Tudor kings. They visit places once ravaged by plagues and fires and falling bombs. They walk where William Shakespeare, Samuel Pepys and Charles Dickens once walked.

They see an ancient city full of modern wonders.

Today, sleek new office buildings dominate London's skyline.

Timeline

43 – Romans found the town of Londinium

60 – Londinium destroyed by Boudicca's army

600 – Saxons settle in London

1065 – Westminster Abbey completed

1075 – The White Tower (part of the Tower of London) is built

1348 – The Black Death ravages London

1540 – London's monasteries are torn down

Around 1600 – Shakespeare's plays performed at the Globe

1605 – The Gunpowder Plot

1649 – King Charles I executed in Westminster

1665 – The Great Plague

1666 – The Great Fire of London

1708 – New St. Paul's Cathedral is completed

1840 – Work begins on a new Houses of Parliament

1851 – The Great Exhibition is held in Hyde Park

1863 – World's first underground railway opens in London

1940 – London attacked during the Blitz

1953 – Coronation of Queen Elizabeth II at Westminster Abbey

1980s – London's old docks converted into Docklands

2012 – London hosts the Olympic Games for the third time

Usborne Quicklinks
For links to websites where you can see objects from Roman and medieval times, watch video clips about events such as the Great Fire and take virtual tours of London landmarks, go to the Usborne Quicklinks website at www.usborne.com/quicklinks and type in the keywords 'Story of London'. Please read our internet safety guidelines at the Usborne Quicklinks website.